This book belongs to

_____

MY VERY FIRST BOOK OF

PRAYERS

Copyright © 1993 by Educational Publishing Concepts, Inc.,
Wheaton, Illinois

Published in Nashville, Tennessee, by Oliver-Nelson Books, a division of Thomas Nelson, Inc., Publishers and distributed in Canada by Word Communications, Ltd., Richmond, British Columbia.

The Bible version used in this publication is THE NEW KING JAMES VERSION. Copyright © 1979, 1980, 1982, Thomas Nelson, Inc., Publishers.

Printed in the United States of America.

Library of Congress Cataloging-in-Publication Data

Hollingsworth, Mary, 1947–
    My very first book of prayers / Mary Hollingsworth : illustrated by Rick Incrocci.
        p.   cm.
    Summary: A collection of simple prayers for different occasions, encouraging the use of prayer for any reason at any time.
        ISBN 0-8407-9229-8 (hardback)
    1. Prayers—Juvenile literature. 2. Children—Prayer-books and devotions—English.   [1. Prayers. 2. Prayer books and devotions.]
I. Incrocci, Rick, ill. II. Title.
BV265.H64   1993
242'.82—dc20
                                                        93-7291
                                                           CIP
                                                            AC

1 2 3 4 5 6 — 98 97 96 95 94 93

MY VERY FIRST BOOK OF

PRAYERS

Mary Hollingsworth

Illustrated by
Rick Incrocci

THOMAS NELSON PUBLISHERS
Nashville

Dear Parents,

Prayer is talking to God. Talking to God can sound a little scary to a young child. But God is waiting for your child to talk to Him. He loves His children so much that he wants to listen to them talk to Him often.

We need to help young children learn that prayer is a special present that God gave to us a long time ago. People have been happily talking to Him ever since. God is not something to fear but someone to love, someone to laugh with, someone to cry with, someone to protect us and care for us.

This book will help you teach your child
how to talk to God without fear. The prayers are
for special times in your child's life. You'll see
prayers for home and church, for happy times
and sad times. That's because your child can talk
to God anywhere, anytime, all the time.

God is always listening. Why not help your
child learn to talk to Him right now? Along the
way, you might learn to be a little more
comfortable talking to God, too.

Mary Hollingsworth

Prayers for My Family

Dear Lord,

Please help my mama. She is a
good mama. I love her so much. My
mama works hard, God. Sometimes she
gets tired. Please help her get lots of
sleep tonight. Thank You for giving me
such a good mom, Lord. I love You.

In Jesus' name,
Amen

For My Mama

Dear God,

I really love my daddy. He is big and strong. He takes good care of us. I want to be just like my daddy someday, Lord. Please take care of him. Help Daddy be just like You.

In Jesus' name,
Amen

For My Daddy

Dear Father,

Thanks for giving me a brother to play with. Playing with him is a lot better than playing by myself. I know we sometimes fight. I am really sorry for that, Lord. Please help me learn to share with him more. Help us be good friends.

In Jesus' name,
Amen

For My Brother

Dear Father,

I really love my sister. She helps me learn things. She plays with me. Please forgive me when I am mean to her or tease her. Please help me do nice things for her. Thanks for my sister, Lord.

In Jesus' name,
Amen

For My Sister

Dear God,

Thank You for giving me such a good grandmother. She always does nice things for me. She bakes cookies and reads stories. She has lots of time just for me. I love her, God. I am glad You do, too.

In Jesus' name,
Amen

For My Grandmother

Dear Lord,

I have the best grandfather in the whole world. He is never too busy for me. I know he loves me. His eyes twinkle when he sees me. I think he is a lot like You. I love him, God. Please help me think to tell him tomorrow.

In Jesus' name,
Amen

For My Grandfather

Prayers for
Other People

Dear Lord,

Thank You so much for letting Jesus come to earth. He was so kind and good. I want to be like that, too. Lord, please help me be the best I can be. I want You to be proud of me. I love You.

In Jesus' name,
Amen

For Jesus

Dear God,

I love to learn about You and Jesus. My Sunday school teacher makes learning so much fun. She is nice. I know she loves You a lot. Please help me listen when my teacher talks. Please help me learn as much as I can. Maybe I can teach others about You someday, too.

In Jesus' name,
Amen

For My Teacher

31

Dear Father,

Going to church was nice today. My minister shook my hand and smiled at me. I like my minister. He is kind and gentle. He always helps people. Please bless my minister, Lord. Please teach me to help people the way he does.

In Jesus' name,
Amen

For My Minister

Dear Lord,

My best friend is so much fun! We play for hours. We never fuss. We like the same toys. We like the same foods. We like the same games. We even like the same kinds of clothes. Thanks for making good friends, God. They are a great idea!

In Jesus' name,
Amen

For My Best Friend

Prayers for Festive Occasions

Good Morning, Lord,

Today is my birthday. I am so excited! We are having a party. All my friends are coming. Thanks for being a part of my party. And thanks for letting me be born.

In Jesus' name,
Amen

For My Birthday

Dear Father,

I really like to celebrate Easter. My teacher said we have Easter to remember when Jesus came back to life. She said it means we can be saved. We also get to live with You someday. I like that part best. Thank You for Jesus, Lord. I love You.

In Jesus' name,
Amen

For Easter Day

Dear Lord,

Our country has a birthday today. I think it is pretty old. July 4 is the date when our country became free. Thank You for our freedom, God. Now we can worship You without being afraid. We love You, Lord.

In Jesus' name,
Amen

For Independence Day

43

Dear God,

Thank You for the good things You give us every day. Thank You for our food. Thank You for our clothes. Thank You for our homes. Thank You for our family. Thank You for Jesus. Thank You for the church. Thank You for loving us. Thank You, God, for saving us. Thank You for everything!

In Jesus' name,
Amen

For Thanksgiving Day

Dear Father,

Today is Christmas. I am so happy! It is the best day of the year. It is the day Jesus was born. Everybody hugs and laughs and sings. I wish Christmas lasted all year long. I love You, God. Merry Christmas! Happy birthday, Jesus.

In Your name,
Amen

For Christmas Day

Dear Lord,

This is the first day of the new year. Thank You for today. Please bless my mom and dad this year. Please take care of me. We love You, Lord. Help us tell other people about Jesus this year.

In His name,
Amen

For New Year's Day

Prayers for
Giving Thanks

Dear Father,

Thank You for the sunshine today. Sunshine makes me feel warm. It makes me happy. I think the flowers and trees like the sunshine, too. Sunshine was a great idea, Lord!

In Jesus' name,
Amen

For Sunshine

Dear Lord,

You made so many pretty things. I think I like the flowers best. They look so pretty. They smell so nice. I like all the colors! Thanks for making flowers, Lord. They make me happy when I see them.

In Jesus' name,
Amen

For Flowers

Dear God,

Who taught the birds their songs? Was it You? I like to hear them sing. I love to look at the pretty butterflies. I wish I could hold one. Thank You for creatures that fly, Father. You did a good job making them.

In Jesus' name,
Amen

For Creatures That Fly

Dear God,

You must have had a lot of fun making all the animals. I like their stripes and polka dots. I like their funny sounds. Thanks for all the animals, God. Help me be gentle with them.

In Jesus' name,
Amen

For Creatures That
Do Not Fly

Dear Father,

It is fun to play outside in the rain. Rain makes neat puddles and mud pies. The flowers and grass like the rain, too. Their colors get prettier after the rain. How did You think of making rain, God? You must be very smart. Thanks for the rain!

In Jesus' name,
Amen

For Rain

Dear Lord,

My family is really happy today. We are going on vacation! Please bless us as we go. Keep us safe and well. Help us all have fun. Help us learn to love each other more. I am glad You go along with us. Thank You for vacations.

In Jesus' name,
Amen

For Vacation

Dear Father,

Thank You for making my body strong. Thank You for making me healthy. I can run and jump and play. I can sing and work. I know some children are sick a lot. That must be hard. Please help me be kind to them. I love You, Lord. You are so good to me.

In Jesus' name,
Amen

For My Healthy Body

Prayers for
Help

Dear Lord,

I do not feel good today. I need You to help me feel better. Please help me rest. Please help me get well. Until then, please help me not be too fussy. Thank You for being with me, Lord.

In Jesus' name,
Amen

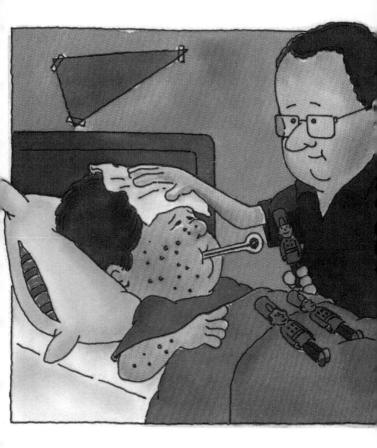

When I Am Sick

Dear God,

I guess You know I am in the hospital. It is not a very fun place to be. I hope I can go home soon. God, please help the nurses and doctors make me well. I know they cannot do it without You. God, could You make it soon?

In Jesus' name,
Amen

When I Am in
the Hospital

Dear Father,

I don't know much about death. All I know is I am sad. Mom says that is because I miss the person who died. I guess that is true. Please take good care of _____ for us. Please help me understand about what happened a little better. We love You, Lord.

In Jesus' name,
Amen

When Someone Dies

Dear Lord,

I am a little scared right now. Thunder and lightning scare me. I know You are taking care of things. Please protect us from the storm. If You don't mind, Lord, could You make it a little quieter so I can sleep? Thank You.

In Jesus' name,
Amen

When I Am Scared

Dear God,

You know I am a little worried about tomorrow. I want to be big and brave. That is not how I feel. Please help me not be so afraid. I am glad You will be with me tomorrow. Could You ask my mom or dad to go with me, too?

In Jesus' name,
Amen

When I Am Worried

Dear Lord,

My pet is lost. I am so worried. I would be sad if something happened to my little friend. Lord, please keep him/her safe for us. Please show us where to find my pet. I know You can do it, God. Thanks for listening.

In Jesus' name,
Amen

When My Pet Is Lost

Prayers For Special Times

Dear God,

Today has been a good day. Thank You for a happy day. Now I need to go to sleep. Please help me have happy dreams. Please take care of my mom and dad. Happy dreams to You, too, Lord! Good night.

In Jesus' name,
Amen

When I Go to Bed

Dear Father,

You have been so good to our family. Thank You for loving us so much. Thank You for our food. Help us share what we have with other people. We know all the good things we have come from You. We love You for that, Father.

In Jesus' name,
Amen

When I Eat

Dear Lord,

I have to go to the doctor today. You know it is not my favorite thing to do, God. I am always a little scared. Please help me remember that the doctor is my friend. The doctor can make me feel better. Please help me be brave and not cry.

In Jesus' name,
Amen

When I Go to the Doctor

Dear God,

We are moving away today. I am excited. I know I will miss my friends. But You will go with us to our new home. So I know it will be okay. I will go now, Lord. Thanks for being with us.

In Jesus' name,
Amen

When I Move Away

Dear Father,

You are the greatest Father of all. You are kind. You are good to me and my family. You give us everything we need. I love You more than anything in the world. Help me grow up to be just like You and Your Son. You are the best.

In Jesus' name,
Amen

When I Want to Praise God

Other books in this series

My Very First Book of Bible Words

My Very First Book of Lessons

My Very First Book of Bible Heroes